100 ELECTRONICS

MINI PROJECTS

Arsath Natheem S

Copyright © 2018 by futurebme.com

WHY I WROTE THIS BOOK

I wrote this book because electronic projects play a vital role in improving skill as well as in increasing career opportunities for a student. Making a project will expose the practical side of a scholar. Project based learning will lead to cooperating education and make a deeper impact on the student. it also creates the knowledge part more enjoyable as students are able to grasp more while learning it in a group. Therefore, let us focus on good projects related to different sectors of electronics and Communication that will enhance one's skills. Project work allows graduates to think out of the case owed to the creative levels of imagination. Right from selecting a topic from an area of interest, this project work involves finding creative solutions to several project associated problems and many technical challenges. Project works at all times make developments to the existing system, and therefore, it ultimately enables students to think socially with an innovative practical mindset and thought. An electronic engineer should implement his knowledge to develop society

"Tell me and I forget, teach me and I may remember, involve me and I learn" -- Benjamin Franklin

WHY YOU SHOULD READ THIS BOOK

The book includes 100 exciting projects in comprehensive functional description and electronic circuits for innovators, engineering students and electronics lover, this book is written for all the people who love innovation. It is the huge collection of ideas to do some innovative project, to create something new. I believe this Book will be helpful for the students for their mini project, also includes functioning basics in case of electronic components i.e., Resistors, Capacitors, Diodes, Transformers, Transistors, LEDs, Variable Resistors, ICs, and PCB. This book for scholars and hobbyists to learn basic electronics through practical presentable circuits. A handy guide for college and school science fair projects or for creation personal hobby, Design new panels and make new circuit designs.

TABLE OF CONTENT

Introduction 1

Basic Electronic Components 1

    Resistors 2

    Capacitors 4

    Inductors 6

    Transformer 6

    Diode 7

    Light emitting diode (LED) 8

    Variable resistor (Potentiometer) 9

    Transistors 10

    Integrated circuit (IC) 11

    H-bridge 13

    Printed Circuit Board (PCB) 14

1. Automatic Water Pump Controller 16
2. Little Power-Hila Vinegar Battery to power a calculator 16
3. Night Vision Enhancer 17
4. Emergency Photo Lamp 20
5. 1W LED For Automotive Applications 20
6. Play with Robotic Eye (IR Sensor) 2
7. Faulty Car Indicator Alarm 22

8. Long-range Burglar Alarm Using Laser Torch 23

9. Soldering Iron Temperature Controller 24

10. Make your own Electric Bug Zapper 25

11. Timer for Mosquito Destroyer 26

12. Radiation Sensor 27

13. Handy Tester 27

14. Strain Meter 28

15. Water Pump Controller 29

16. Timer with Musical Alarm 30

17. Simple Key-hole Lighting Device 30

18. Ball Speed Checker 31

19. Halogen lamp Saver for Bikes 32

20. HDD Selector Switch 32

21. Simple Key-Operated Gate Locking System 33

22. Mains Box Heat Monitor 34

23. Digital Soil Moisture Test 34

24. Over-Heating Indicator for Water Pipe 35

25. Linear Timer for General Use 36

26. Noise Meter 36

27. Mains Failure and Resumption Alarm 38

28. Multipurpose White-LED Light 38

29. IR-Based Light Control 39

30. Sequential Device Control using TV Remote Control 40

31. Software of the Month: Resistor Calculator 1.0.6 41

32. IR-Controlled Water Supply 41

33. Triple-Mode Tone Generator 42

34. Twilight Lamp Blinker 44

35. Electronic Street Light Switch 44

36. Standby Power-Loss Preventer 45

37. Touch Alarm 45

38. Hum-Sensitive Touch Alarm 46

39. Room Sound Monitor 47

40. Security System Switcher 47

41. Doorbell-controlled Security Switch 48

42. Pencell Charge Indicator 49

43. Power Resumption Alarm and Low-Voltage Protector 50

44. Miser Flash 50

45. Automatic Soldering Iron Switch 51

46. White LED Light Probe for Inspection 52

47. Calling Bell Using an Intercom 52

48. FM Bug 54

49. Digital Frequency Comparator 54

50.	Bhajan and Mantra Chanting amplifier	55
51.	Quality FM Transmitter	56
52.	Mains Box Heat Monitor	57
53.	Tachometer	57
54.	Timer from Old Quartz Clock	58
55.	Keep Away Ni-Cd from Memory effect	59
56.	Periodically on off Mosquito ad hoc circuit	59
57.	Crystal AM Transmitter	60
58.	Programmable Electronic Dice	61
59.	PC-Based Candle Igniter	61
60.	Sound Operated Intruder Alarm	62
61.	Versatile LED Display	63
62.	Multiutility flash light	64
63.	Twilight using white LEDs	64
64.	PC TIMER	65
65.	Infrared Object Counter	65
66.	Pushbutton Control for Single-Phase Appliances	66
67.	Soldering Iron Tip preserver	67
68.	Over-Speed Indicator	68
69.	Automatic Washbasin Tap Controller	68
70.	1.5W Power Amplifier	69

71. Wireless Stepper Motor Controllers 70
72. Battery-Low Indicator 70
73. Speed Checker for Highways 71
74. Simple Stereo Level Indicator 72
75. Manual EPROM Programmer 73
76. Noise-Muting FM Receiver 74
77. PC-Based Stepper Motor Controller..74
78. Digital Audio/Video Input Selector..75
79. Automatic Bathroom Light with Back-up Lamp............................76
80. Simple Low-Power Inverter 76
81. Mains Interruption Counter with Indicator...................................77
82. FM Adaptor for Car Stereo 78
83. Panic Plate...78
84. Twinkle X-mas Star 79
85. Car Fan Speed Controller 80
86. In Car Food and Beverage Warmer 80
87. Three Component Flasher...81
88. Night Lamp 82
89. Hot-Water-Ready Alarm 82
90. Optical Smoke Detector...83
91. Capacitance-Multiplier Power Supply...84

92.	Wireless PA for Classrooms	84
93.	Low-Cost Battery Charger	85
94.	Simple Automatic Water-Level Controller	86
95.	Touch-Plate Doorbell	86
96.	Electronic Ludo	87
97.	Motorbike Alarm	88
98.	Dual Motor Control for Robots	89
99.	Environment Monitoring System Using Arduino	90
100.	Long-Range IR Transmitter	92
	MORE USEFUL LINKS	93
	References	97

Introduction

An overview to electronic components which is used to make more innovative projects There are numerous basic electrical and electronic components are normally found in numerous circuits of peripherals such as hard-disk, mother boards, etc. Several circuits are designed with numerous components like resistors, capacitors, transistors, inductors, transformers, fuses and switches etc. Therefore, this book offers a quick info concerning different types of electronic and electrical components that are utilized in various electronic and electrical projects, embedded systems. Let you will see each and every part in detail with diagrams. Resistors, inductors, transformers

Basic Electronic Components

Major Electrical and Electronic Components The major electrical and electronic components utilized in electrical and electronic projects like resistors, capacitors, transistors, integrated circuits (IC), switches, relays, motors, etc. In many circuits, these components are used to build the innovative projects.

Resistors

A resistor impedes the movement of electricity over a circuit, resistors have a conventional value.

Since voltage, current and resistance are associated over Ohm's law, resistors are a simple technique to control voltage and current in your circuit.

Resistor color codes

1st band = 1st number
2nd band = 2nd number
3rd band = # of zeros / multiplier
4th band = tolerance

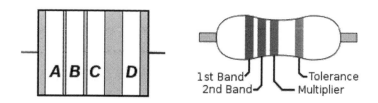

Color Code Number: (BBROYGBVGW)

Tolerance: Gold = within 5%

Black: 0
Brown: 1
Red: 2
Orange: 3
Yellow: 4
Green: 5
Blue: 6
Violet: 7
Gray: 8
White: 9

Unit

- To Identifying your units is significant
- Kilo & Mega are basic in resistors
- Milli, micro, nano & pico can be utilized in additional components

K (kilo) = 1,000
M (mega) = 1,000,000
M (milli) = 1/1,000
u (micro) = 1/1,000,000
n (nano) = 1/1,000,000,000 (one trillionth)
p (pico) = 1/ 1,000,000,000,000 (one quadrillionth)

Capacitors

- A capacitor is used to stores electrical energy. here pool of electrons is obtainable for electronic components to usage.

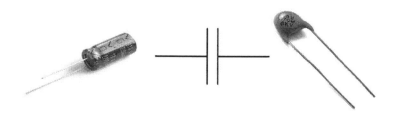

Capacitance is measured in the unit of Farads. The mini capacitors typically used in electronics are often determined in micro-farads and nano-farads. Some capacitors are polarized. Have to know the different length of terminals on one of the capacitors.

Polarity of capacitors

- The smaller terminal goes on the -ive side.
- The strip is on the -ive terminal sideways of the capacitor.

The panel is noted for +ive or -ive.

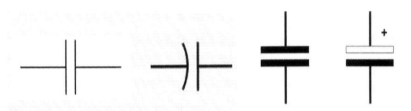

Applications of capacitors

- Capacitors can pass a *pool of electrons* for instant use.
- If a component wants an instantaneous supply of electrons, the capacitor can pass those electrons.

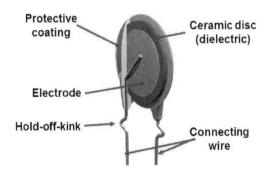

Capacitors can **smooth out a signal** - remove the waves or spikes in DC voltage. The capacitor can attract the peaks and fill in the vales of a waved signal.

Inductors

An inductor is a passive electronic component which is stores energy as a magnetic field. In its minimum tough form, an inductor includes of a wire loop or coil. The inductance is straight proportional to the amount of turns in the coil. Inductance similarly relies upon the distance of the coil and on the kind of material about which the coil is wound.

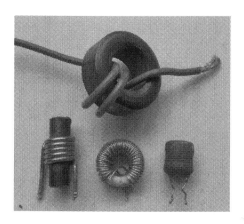

An inductor, similarly called a coil, choke or reactor, is a passive two-terminal electrical component which stores the current in a magnetic-field once electric current pass through it. An inductor usually includes of an insulated wire twisted into a coil about a centre.

Transformer

A transformer is a static-electrical device which exchanges electrical current among at minimum two circuits over electromagnetic acceptance. A changing current in one coil of the transformer makes an opposing magnetic field, that thusly prompts a shifting electromotive force (emf) or "voltage" in a instant coil. Energy can be exchanged among the two coils, without a metallic suggestion between the two circuits.

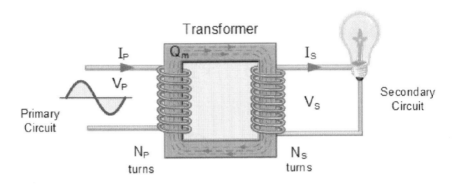

Faraday's law of inductance found in 1831 portrayed this influence. Transformers are utilized to increment or lessening the rotating voltages in electric energy applications.

Diode

- A diode is a one-way controller (or gate) for electricity. Diode is a component by an irregular transfer characteristic.
- A diode has little (preferably zero) resistance in one way, and high (preferably infinite) resistance in the other way.

- Diodes will protect your electronics

Diode circuit protection

In a DPDT switch, if polarization is incorrect, the motor will run backwards. In an electronic circuit, if the polarization is incorrect, you can fry your components.

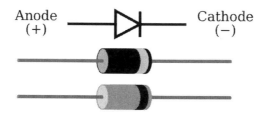

A diode in your scheme will assistance to avoid problems.

Light emitting diode (LED)

A light emitting diode (LED) is a semiconductor light source. Once electricity is flow through the diode, it produces light.

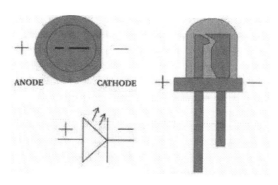

Variable resistor (Potentiometer)

A potentiometer is a variable resistor. As you physically turn a dial, the resistance variations.

How a variable resistor works

As the dial or wiper turns, electricity essential go through more or less of the resistive strip.

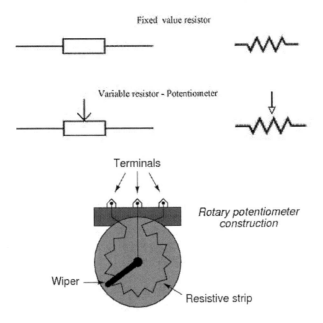

In sequence, the variation in resistance means a variation in voltage, so as you turn the dial or wiper, you become a variation in voltage

Transistors

A transistor is a semiconductor device applicable to switch and amplify electrical power and electronic signals.

How a transistor works

- A voltage or current pass to one pair of the transistor's terminals variations the current over different pair of terminals.
- A transistor is combines of semiconductor material with at minimum three terminals, for assembly to an external circuit.

Transistors have 3 pins.

1. Collector
2. Emitter
3. Base

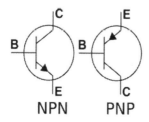

Schematic symbols

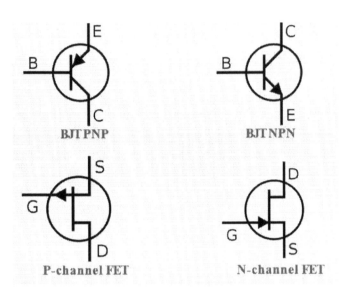

Integrated circuit (IC)

- An integrated circuit (IC) is a group of transistors which is the controller or 'brain' of an electronic circuit.
- An input is received, an output is sent out.

Current microprocessor ICs can have billions of transistors each square inch

What an IC can do for us?

- Billions of electronically measured on/off switches (transistors) is how the microprocessor in a digital computer 'thinks' and purposes.
- A computer has a wide variety of tasks to perform.
- But other ICs can fully simpler, separate jobs. For i.e., an IC can take a voltage input and output instructions to a motor.

IC Terminology: Op-amp

An operational amplifier (op-amp) is a group of transistors inside the IC (Integrated Circuit). They frequently are the components doing the mathematical procedures.

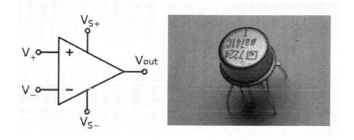

H-bridge

An electronic circuit which allows voltage to be applied across a load in any direction.

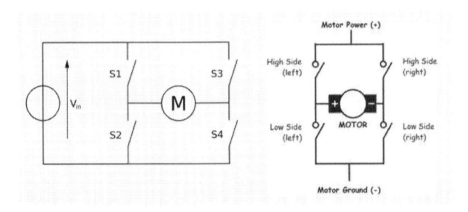

A DPDT switch also does this, but not electronically

Varying voltage

- A potentiometer or variable resistor permits you to variation the voltage input which goes into the integrated circuit (IC).
- Integrated circuit can now output change of pulse widths to the transistors on the H-bridge.

- This grouping of potentiometer, integrated circuit and PWM to the H-bridge *is **the key to speed controller.***

Printed Circuit Board (PCB)

- The 'front' side of the board will have printed component information, such as resistor and resistance, diode type and polarity, Components are attached to a printed circuit board.

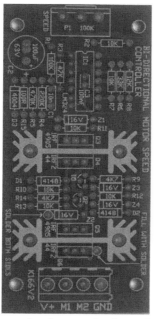

- Holes go all the method over the board since one side to the other. Over hole soldering is needed to join components to the board.

Backside of Circuit Board

- The 'back' side of the board will have lines indicating contacts between components. The lines on the back are alike to wires.
- Denser lines denote extra current (electrons) moving through.

- Components connect the lines.

Conclusion

- Confidently that wasn't too confusing.
- The aim was to give you a simple understanding of how about of the electronic components of a motor speed controller work.
- Here's lots of tools to help you with the basics.

1. Automatic Water Pump Controller

This circuit consequently controls the water pump motor. The motor gets naturally exchanged on when water in the overhead tank (OHT) falls underneath as far as possible. Additionally, it gets turned off when the tank is topped off. Worked around just a single NAND gate IC number CD4011, the circuit is straightforward, minimized and conservative. It works off a 12V DC power supply and devours next to no power.

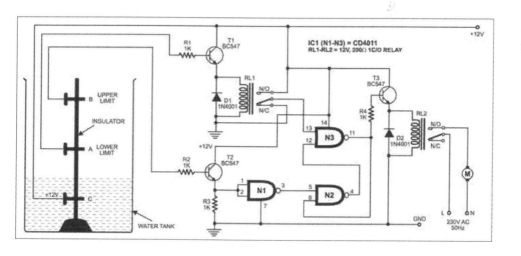

2. Little Power-Hila Vinegar Battery to power a calculator

LCD calculators draw next to no current. This vinegar battery effortlessly runs these projects. Take the back off of a reasonable adding machine, expel the battery broaden the two battery wires out the sides at that point reassemble.

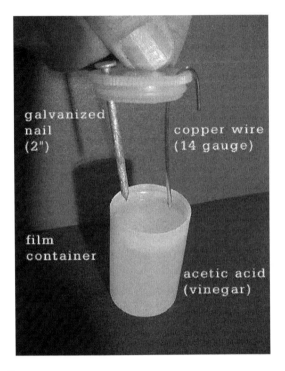

3. Night Vision Enhancer

This is a simple green LED penlight made around 555 timer IC (IC1) and power-driven from a 3V battery pack.

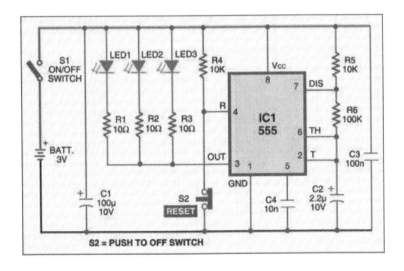

Another circuit

Load shedding is the normal issue in creating nation where understudy is more affected. By remembering this issue, the gathering of dream darling innovation post extremely basic, valuable and economical undertaking utilizing ultra-bright white LEDs which give adequate light to perusing reason which devour low power i.e. 3 watts of power. It works like emergency light i.e. at the point when AC mains disappointment, the battery backup circuit in a flash light up the LEDs yet when the power continues, the battery supply is naturally separated and this circuit again deals with AC mains.

Circuit Explanation of LED-based reading lamp

Power segment the circuit of LED-based perusing light utilize bridge rectifier associated with optional loop of 0-7.5V, 500mA step-down transformer X1. Throbbing DC from yield of rectifier is given to contribution of voltage regulator IC1 for unadulterated DC yield. All LEDs (LED1 to LED10) is associated in parallel across the yield of voltage regulator. Here resistors R1 to R10 are associated in arrangement with the LEDs individually to restrain the current. In this circuit 5 more LEDs can be utilized for light to build power in a similar way utilized. At the point when AC mains accessible hand-off RL1 invigorated and detach to battery and the other way around on truant of AC mains. For charging battery, a lead from rectifier is straightforwardly associated with +ive and - ive terminals of battery. Here diode D5 and D6 is utilized as switch current insurance diode that don't enable the battery current to stream towards the supply segment and diode D7 is for turnaround extremity assurance.

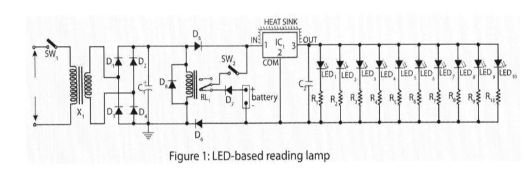

Figure 1: LED-based reading lamp

Components

- Required Resistors (all ¼-watt, ± 5% Carbon)
  R1- R10 = 56 Ω
- Required Capacitors
  C1 = 1000 μF/16V; C2 = 0.1 μF
- Required Semiconductors
  IC1 = 7805 Voltage regulator

4. Emergency Photo Lamp

This emergency lamp can be powered moreover by a rechargeable battery (like 3.6V Ni-Cadmium) or a non-rechargeable battery (3.0V CR2032). The white LED (LED1) gleams certainly once the power comes up short and you are left in dull. The quiescent current of the circuit is low and the battery is for all intentions and purposes utilized just once the LED gleams

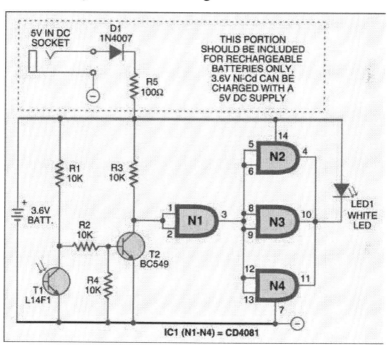

5. 1W LED For Automotive Applications

This easy circuit gives you a chance to run a 1W Light Emitting Diode from the battery of your Vehicle. IC MC34063 is utilized here as a buck converter. It is a solid switching regulator sub-framework planned for use as a DC-DC converter. The projects comprise of an inner temperature-repaid reference, a comparator, a controlled obligation cycle oscillator with a dynamic ebb and flow restrict circuit, a driver and a high-ebb and flow yield switch. These capacities are contained in an 8-stick double in-line bundle. Another real favourable position of the switching regulator is that it permits expanded application adaptability of the yield voltage.

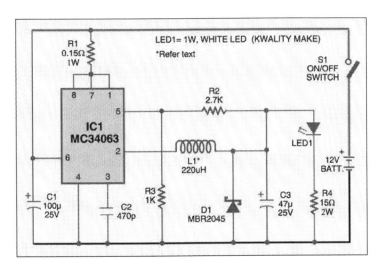

6. Play with Robotic Eye (IR Sensor)

There are different uses of IR sensors, for example, TV remote controllers, criminal alerts and protest counters. Here we have utilized IR sensors (infrared LEDs) to influence a question identification to circuit and furthermore a proximity sensor for way following robots. The fundamental thought is to transmit the infrared light through an IR LED, which is then reflected by any snag ahead and detected by the getting LED.

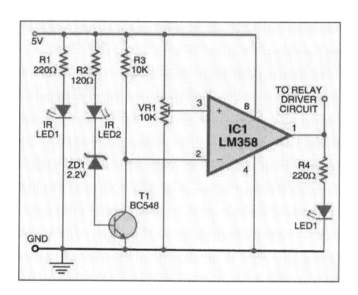

7. Faulty Car Indicator Alarm

Before going ahead, either left or right, auto drivers need to switch on the auto turn indicator lights with the goal that the moving toward vehicle drivers can avoid potential risk as needs be. An accident is probably going to happen on the off chance that your auto turns indicator lights neglect to glow because of some reason or the other. Here is a circuit that sounds an alert if your turn indicator lights don't glow, helping you to protect against any accident.

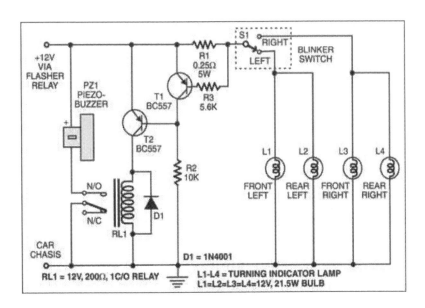

8. Long-range Burglar Alarm Using Laser Torch

Laser burn based robber alarms typically work in haziness as it were. In any case, this long-extend photoelectric alarm can work dependably in daytime additionally to caution you against interlopers in your huge compounds, and so on. The alarm includes laser transmitter and receiver units, which are to be mounted on the contrary mainstays of the passage gate. At whatever point anybody enters to intrude on the transmitted laser bar falling on the receiver, the buzzer in the receiver circuit sounds an alarm.

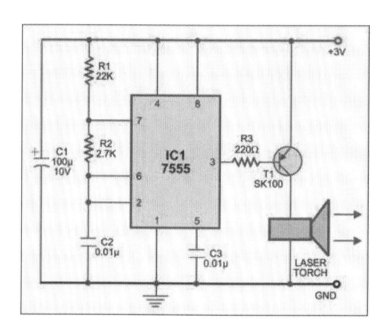

9. Soldering Iron Temperature Controller

This is an easy circuit to control the temperature of a soldering iron. It is particularly helpful if the soldering iron is to be kept on for since a long time ago you can control the heat dispersal from the iron. At the point when a soldering iron is exchanged on, the iron sets aside opportunity to achieve the patch's liquefying point. Basically, associate this circuit to the soldering iron as appeared in the figure and the iron achieves the weld's liquefying point rapidly.

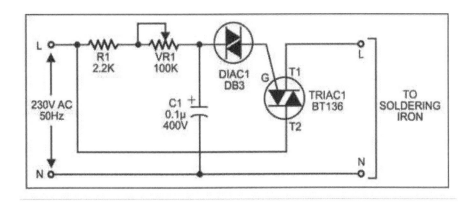

10. Make your own Electric Bug Zapper

None of us prefers bugs at home. To murder these flying creepy crawlies, they should first be pulled in and after that electrocuted. Bug zapper is one such gadget with a high-voltage shocking circuit and a creepy crawly drawing in UV lamp of 365 nm wavelength. This ultraviolet fluorescent lamp is mounted amidst the bureau and a couple of painstakingly divided, electrically protected, charged wire networks encompass the light. At the point when a creepy crawly approach enough to the work match, an electrical circular segment is framed, the dielectric breakdown and current flows through the bug's body. Shocking the creepy crawly doesn't expect it to touch both the wires as a bend frames noticeable all-around hole more than 1800V.

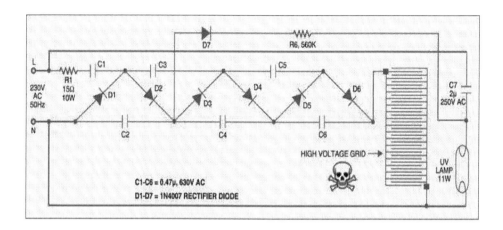

11. Timer for Mosquito Destroyer

In electric-heating mosquito anti-agents, an electric vaporizer warms up a tangle or fluid to discharge non-debasing chemicals into the air and ward off the mosquitoes from the shut environment. Here's a circuit that presents a period hole in the task of the of 15 minutes without lessening the anti-agent's activity on mosquitoes.

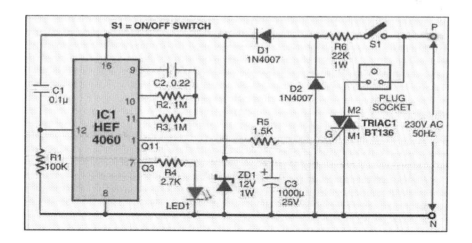

12. Radiation Sensor

When you take a shot at a PC or stare at the TV, your body is overwhelmed in an electronic brown haze radiating from the device. For example, in CRT-based monitors, the spot of electrons that range the screen creates beat electromagnetic radiation . A portion of this energy escapes as radiations in low-frequency and to a great degree low-frequency energy.

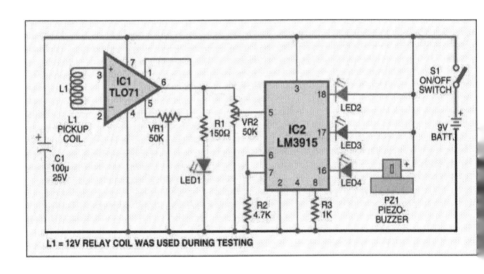

13. Handy Tester

For novices, here is a minimal effort multitester that can be utilized to test the state of all the electronic components from resistors to ICs. It utilizes just a couple of components however can likewise recognize extremity, coherence, logic states and action of multivibrators.

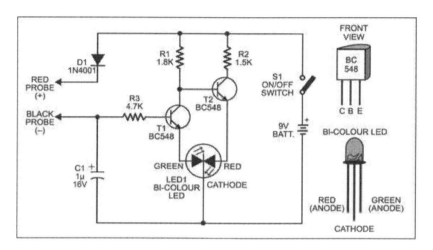

14. Strain Meter

This strain meter demonstrates whether the strain is compressive (decreasing the length) or tractable (expanding the length) when a question, for example, a swagger on a crane changes its shape. The strain is detected by a strain gauge that is stuck to the question being tried. The change in resistance of the strain gauge delivers a change in the perusing of the meter. For the reason, a simple or digital meter, for example, a voltmeter, can be utilized that has full-scale avoidance of 1V DC. Be that as it may, utilization of a digital multimeter would be better.

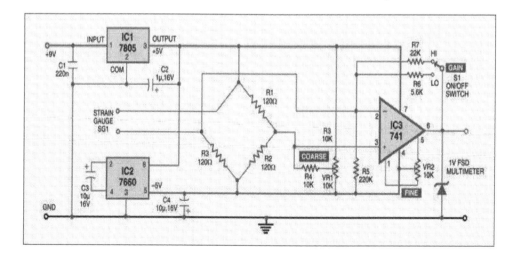

15. Water Pump Controller

Here is a basic circuit for controlling water level in an overhead tank. The fundamental parts of this pump controller are a step-down transformer, a 24V AC double changeover relay, two buoys and two micro switches. Any accessible relay can be utilized independent of its coil voltage. Obviously, current rating of contacts ought to be considered according to the engine control. The relay ought to have two contacts. A step-down transformer having optional voltage suited to the coil voltage of the relay is utilized. As the circuit works off AC, no amendment is fundamental. Micro-switches S1 and S2 settled over the water tank are worked by independent buoys: one for detecting the bot tom level and the other for top level. A three-center wire is utilized for associating these switches to the relay.

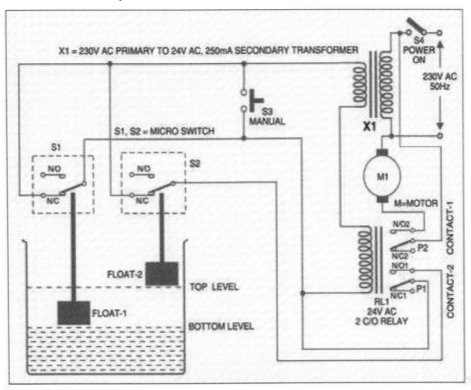

16. Timer with Musical Alarm

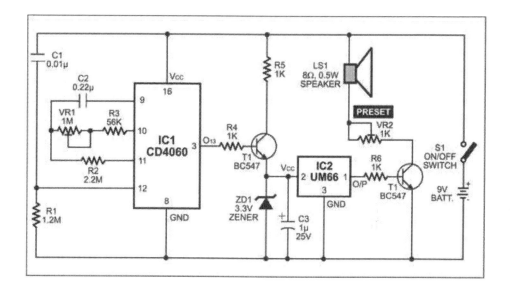

This minimal effort timer can be utilized for presenting a deferral of one moment to two hours. After the planning time frame is more than, a musical melody is heard.

17. Simple Key-hole Lighting Device

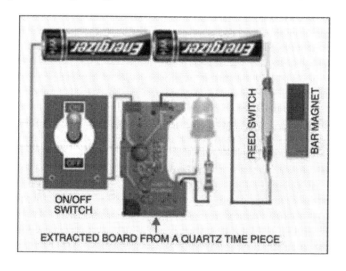

This basic circuit is a extracted circuit load up from a disposed of quartz timepiece.

18. Ball Speed Checker

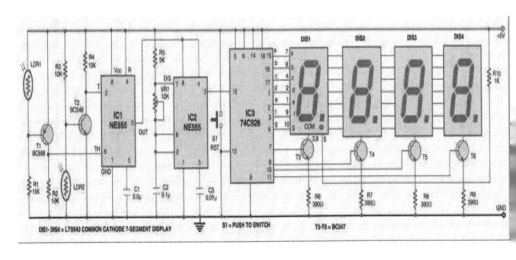

This circuit measures the speed of a cricket ball in light of the time taken by the ball to venture to every part of the separation from the bowling crease to the batting crease.

19. Halogen lamp Saver for Bikes

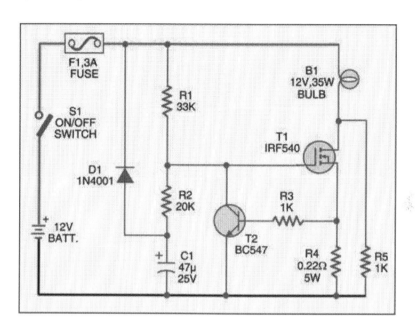

Halogen lamps are inclined to wear out attributable to their minimal cold current. The fast heating inside the lamp melts the thin fiber and stops the lamp life. The circuit depicted here improves the life of the halogen lamp by permitting delicate turn-on of the lamp.

20. HDD Selector Switch

Utilizing the switch-mode power supply (SMPS) of your personal PC, this add-on circuit gives you a chance to switch between three hard disk drives (HDDs) and furthermore guarantee that no one else can open your insured HDD. It is very valuable for protection from hacking and spying.

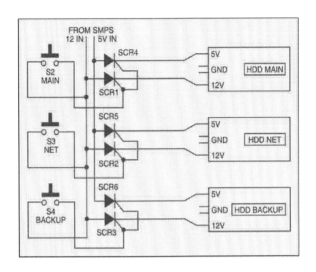

21. Simple Key-Operated Gate Locking System

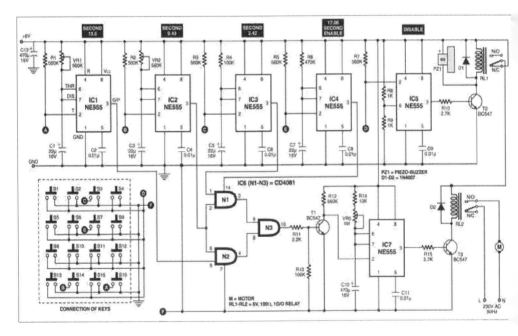

This simple key-operated gate locking system permits just those people who know the preset code to open the gate. The code is to be entered from the keypad inside the preset time to work the motor fitted in the gate. On the off chance that anybody attempting to open the gate presses a wrong key in the keypad, the system is incapacitated and, in the meantime, sounds an alarm to alert you of an unapproved section.

22. Mains Box Heat Monitor

This simple circuit monitors the mains distribution box constantly and sounds an alarm when it senses a high temperature due to overheating, helping to prevent disasters caused by any sparking in the mains box due to short circuits. It also automatically switches on a bright white LED when the power fails. The LED gives ample light to check the mains box wiring or fuses in darkness. The circuit beeps once when power fails and again when power resumes

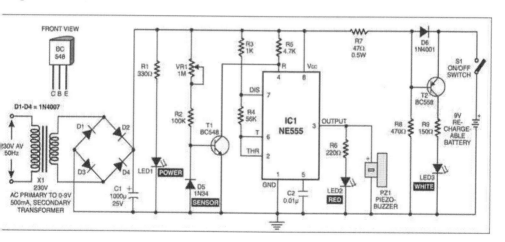

23. Digital Soil Moisture Test

This is a basic and reduced digital soil moisture tester to check whether the soil is dry or wet. It can likewise be utilized to check the dryness or wetness of cotton, woolen and woven textures.

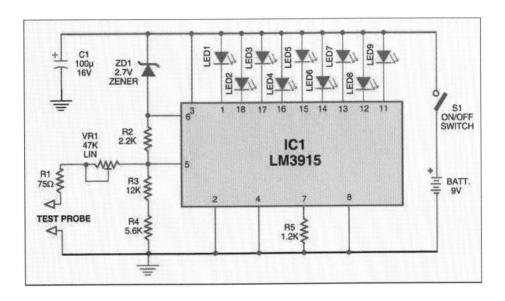

24. Over-Heating Indicator for Water Pipe

The boiling water pipe from the water geyser of your restroom may blast on the off chance that it gets overheated and is left unattended. This circuit monitors the temperature of the water pipe. In the event that the temperature of the pipe goes over certain cutoff, it flashes a LED.

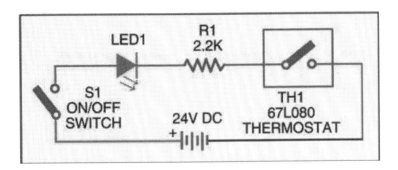

25. Linear Timer for General Use

This basic timer can be used to control any electrical machine that should be switched off after certain time, similar to a little warmer or an evaporator, gave the 'relay switch' parameters meet the prerequisites of that apparatus. It uses minimal effort parts and joins digital accuracy with straightforward simple control, giving long timing spans without the use of high esteemed resistors or capacitors.

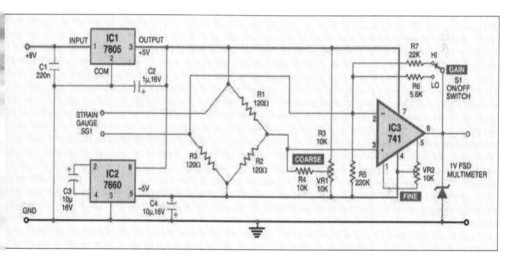

26. Noise Meter

Noise pollution is watches out for some non-communicable diseases and. Safe level of noise is considered up to 30 dBs. This is an intriguing circuit by dream lover technology, "Noise Meter" used to quantify the level of noise arraigning by LED and likewise it gives cautioning when noise crosses the protected level of 30 dB by beeping sound.

Circuit depiction of Noise Meter

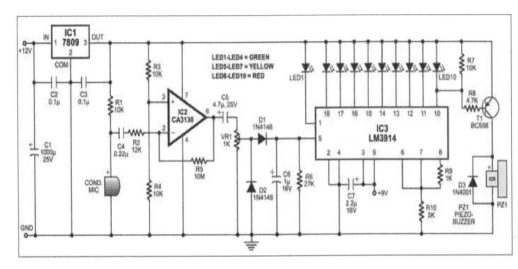

The whole circuit of noise meter has been outlined and manufactured utilizing sound intensity sensor and display unit. This condenser microphone is utilized as sensor of noise meter with operational amplifier (IC2) and relating passive components. The inverting and non-inverting input is given to operational amplifier IC (IC2) from pin 2 and pin 3 separately. Where yield from pin 6 of IC2 is associated with the inverting input for negative feedback through resistor R5. The controlling sound air conditioning signal from potentiometer VR1 is first rectified by diode (D1 and D2) and keeps up it at the yield level of IC2.

The display unit is composed around solid IC LM3914 (IC3). It drives ten LEDs by detecting simple voltage. Each LED is associated with yield of IC3 speaks to the sound level of 3 dB in plunging request from 18 to 10. The gleaming each of the ten LEDs show sound intensity is 30dB.

The PNP transistor get base bias when yield at pin 10 of IC3 goes low to drive the piezo buzzer keeping in mind the end goal to give sound.

Typically, sound intensity up to 30 dB is charming. Over 80 dB, it winds up irritating. What's more, on the off chance that it goes past 100 dB, it might influence your psychomotor execution, degrading your consideration and causing pressure. Noise pollution may likewise influence your listening ability capacity

27. Mains Failure and Resumption Alarm

This mains indicator sounds an alarm at whatever point AC mains falls flat or resumes. It is extremely helpful in mechanical establishments, silver screen theatre hall, multi-specialist's hospitals, and so on.

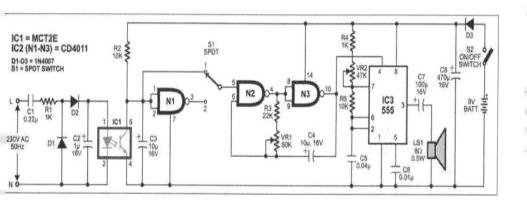

28. Multipurpose White-LED Light

Standard fluorescent lamps and their littler forms called compact fluorescent lamps (CFLs) emanate light every which way (360°) and tend to expand the Hall temperature. In emergency lights utilizing these lamps, the battery keeps going just a couple of hours because of the power misfortune amid transformation of DC into air conditioning. These confinements can be overwhelmed by utilizing ultra-bright white LEDs

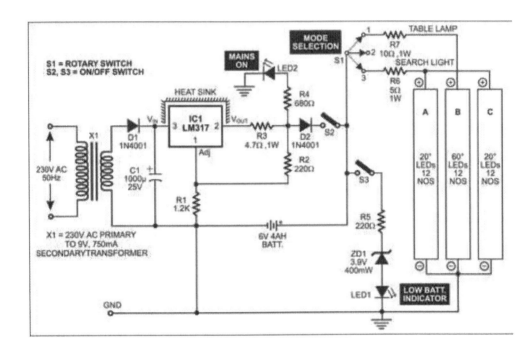

29. IR-Based Light Control

This circuit turns on the lights at the patio, car stopping or different territories when a motorbike or car enters through the gate to cross the detecting zone. It can likewise be utilized as an electronic watchdog for your home, by actuating an alarm at the same time.

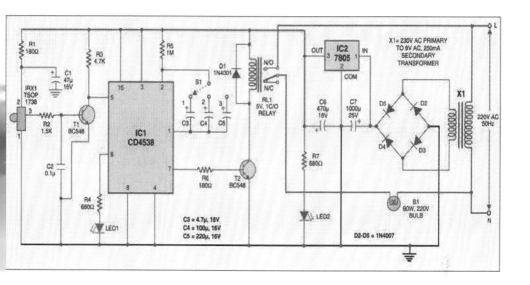

30. Sequential Device Control using TV Remote Control

Here's the circuit gives you a chance to switch on and switch off up to nine devices sequentially from your TV remote control.

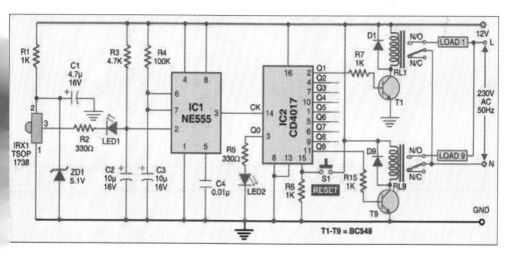

31. Software of the Month: Resistor Calculator 1.0.6

A basic, simple to-utilize freeware for Windows that spares a great deal of time and exertion in deciding the shading code of resistors and resistance esteems required for LED circuits.

Resistor Calculator 1.0.6

Presented here is a simple, easy-to-use freeware for Windows that saves a lot of time and effort in determining the colour code of resistors and resistance values required for LED circuits

DILIN ANAND

Every resistor is marked with colour bands that indicate its resistance, tolerance and sometimes temperature coefficient as well. You might be familiar with the mnemonics for memorising the resistor colour coding: *B. B. ROY of Great Britain has a Very Good Wife*, where the capitalised letters stand for black, brown, red, orange, yellow, green, blue, violet, grey and white, respectively.

Quite often, the whole mental calculation process of resistor codes can be an exhausting task. It also consumes much time. Sometimes you may not remember the mnemon-

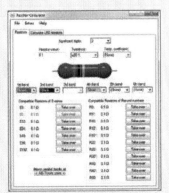

Fig 1: Home screen of resistor calculator

License type	Freeware
Developer	Andreas Breitschopp, AB-Tools.com
Operating system	Windows 8, Windows 7, Windows Vista and Windows XP
Latest version	1.0.6
File size	1.29 MB

interface is clear and plain, which

is a freeware. The users get the latest updates of this program automatically. All updates are absolutely free.

The integrated help system is simple and easy to understand. It also has an intuitive program interface. Further help and support is provided by e-mail and is also available at their website. The program is currently

32. IR-Controlled Water Supply

This circuit can be utilized as a part of homes or little eateries for a water supply unit, for example, Restroom flush or washbasin tap.

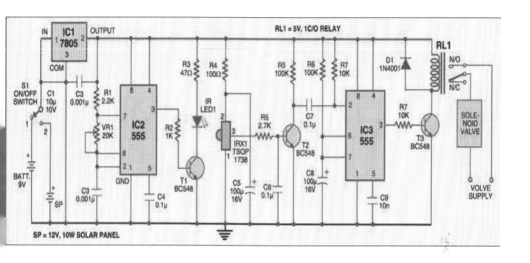

33. Triple-Mode Tone Generator

This is a basic circuit that generates three unique tones. You can utilize it as a call bell, criminal alarm or some other security alarm.

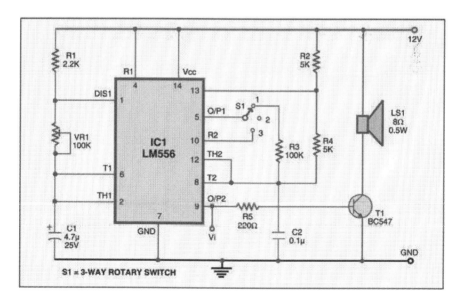

Alternative circuit.

Presently, this is unique tone generator circuit which produces three diverse sorts of sound as per input three distinctive logic levels (i.e. 0&1, 1&0 and 1&1).

Circuit description

This circuit is planned around computerized IC 7400 which is NAND gate. The working of the circuit resembles the working standard of oscillator circuit, where frequency relies on capacitors C1 and C2. The duty cycle of this circuit is half. The yield is given to power amplifier circuit which additionally drive amplifier or earphone. For low frequency estimation of capacitor C1 and C2 must be high and the other way around.

Components

- Required Resistors (all ¼-watt, ± 5% Carbon)
- R1, R4 = 1.2 KΩ; R2, R3 = 1 KΩ; R5 = 10 KΩ; R6, R7 = 47 KΩ
- Required Capacitors
- C1 = 100 kpF; C2 = 220 kpF; C3, C4 = 10 kpF
- Semiconductors IC1 = 7400 (NAND gate)

34. Twilight Lamp Blinker

During sunset or sunrise, the ambient light isn't satisfactory to lead you through the open doorway or advance around obstructions. To dodge any setback, here is a twilight lamp blinker that you can put close obstructions.

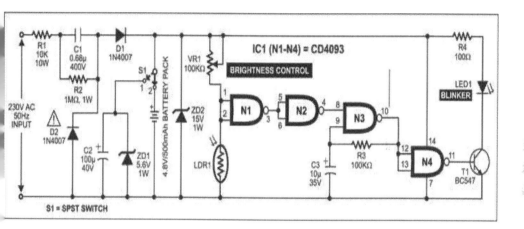

35. Electronic Street Light Switch

This is a easy and minimal effort low cost street light switch. This switch consequently turns on the light at nightfall and turns it off at dawn. The programmed work spares electricity other than man power.

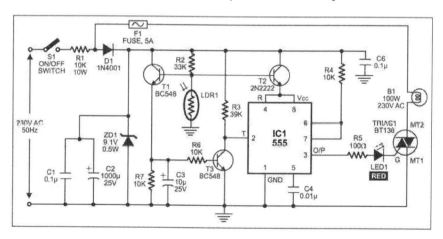

36. Standby Power-Loss Preventer

Electronic devices devour some power even in the standby mode, i.e., when they have been switched off utilizing a remote handset yet not the mains power switch. For example, when a CRT television or PC screen is being used, it devours 80-100 watts of power. In the standby mode as well, it draws a couple of watts of power. Hence in the event that you leave these devices in standby mode for quite a while, they may blow up your electricity bill.

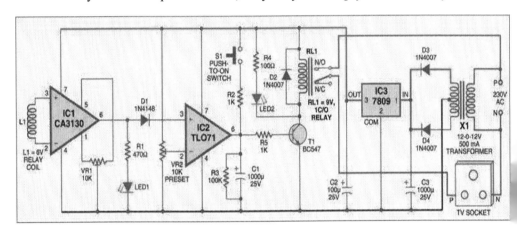

37. Touch Alarm

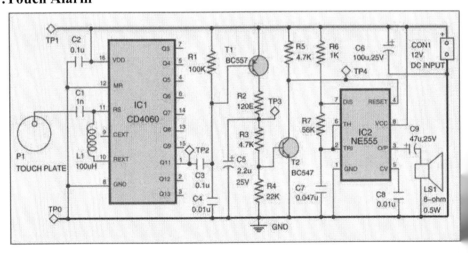

This is a new kind of touch alarm which uses an Radio Frequency oscillator at its input. One unique feature of this touch alarm is that it able to use a big size touch plate. Similarly, no shielded wire is required among the touch plate and the circuit.

58. Hum-Sensitive Touch Alarm

Radiation signals from mains wiring can travel a couple of meters of some distance. These can be instigated by the electromagnetic field in the human body moreover.

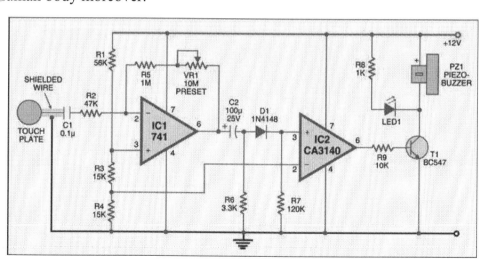

39. Room Sound Monitor

With this basic circuit, you can furtively tune in to conversations going ahead in a room. The circuit is extremely sensitive and powered by a 3V battery.

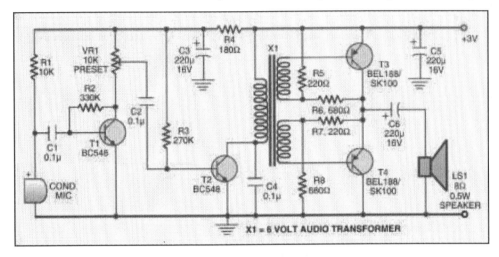

40. Security System Switcher

An audio signal can be utilized as a type of contribution to control any security system. For instance, a programmed security camera can be designed to react to a thump on the entryway. The circuit depicted here enables the security system to programme in on state. It utilizes a transducer to

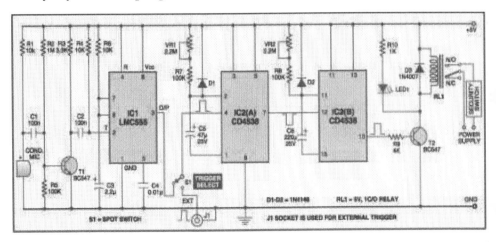

distinguish gate crashers and a 5V controlled DC control supply gives energy to the circuit.

41. Doorbell-controlled Security Switch

One approach to check whether anyone is at home is to ring the doorbell. Robbers too utilize this very strategy. The circuit portrayed here comes helpful in such a circumstance. It is a straightforward doorbell controlled multipurpose security switch that right away powers up an associated security device, say, a night-vision entryway camera, for working. The circuit works off 9V DC supply. The input of the circuit is associated in parallel with the 230V Air conditioning electric doorbell. An electromagnetic relay is utilized at the yield of the circuit to activate the security device associated with it.

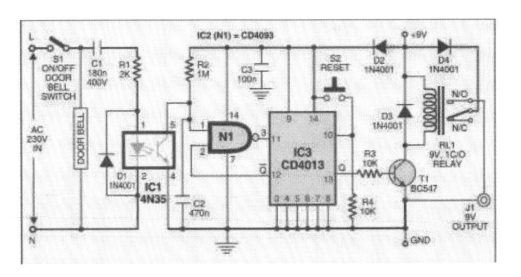

42. Pencell Charge Indicator

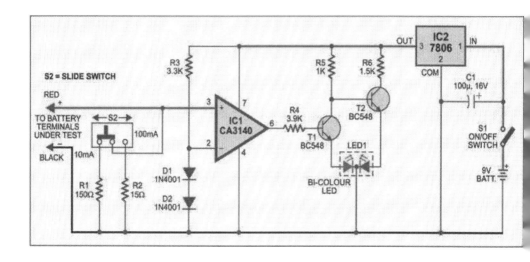

Small size AA cells and button cells utilized as a part of electronic devices giving a terminal voltage of 1.5V are regularly evaluated at 500 mAh. As the cells discharge, their internal impedance increments to frame a potential divider alongside the heap and the battery terminal voltage diminishes. This, thus, lessens the execution of the device and we are compelled to supplant the battery with another one. Be that as it may, a similar battery can be utilized again in some other application that requires less current.

43. Power Resumption Alarm and Low-Voltage Protector

The circuit portrayed here protects your electrical apparatuses like air conditioning motors from harm because of low voltage at power-on. It stays standby without offering power to the load after power resumes. The load can be switched on only physically. This counteracts harm to the device on the off chance that it is 'on' when power resumes.

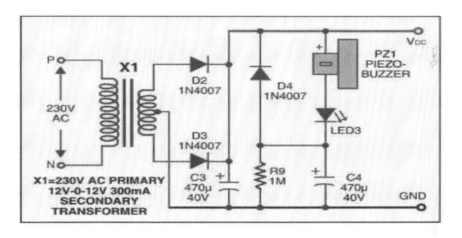

44. Miser Flash

A flashing LED at the doorstep of your carport or home will trap the hoodlums into trusting that an advanced security contraption is installed. The circuit is only a low current drain flasher. It utilizes a solitary CMOS timer that is designed as a free running oscillator utilizing a couple of extra parts. As the LED flashes quickly, the normal current through the LED is around 150 µA with a high peak value, which is adequate for typical review. This makes it a genuine miser.

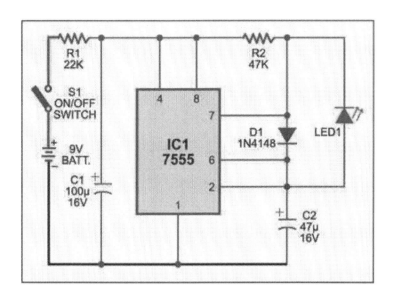

45. Automatic Soldering Iron Switch

Frequently, we forget to turn off the soldering iron. This outcomes in a smoking oxidized iron as well as waste of electricity. To take care of this issue, here is a circuit that automatically switches off the soldering iron after a foreordained time. The circuit draws no power when it is latent. The circuit can likewise be utilized for controlling the electric iron, kitchen timer or different uses.

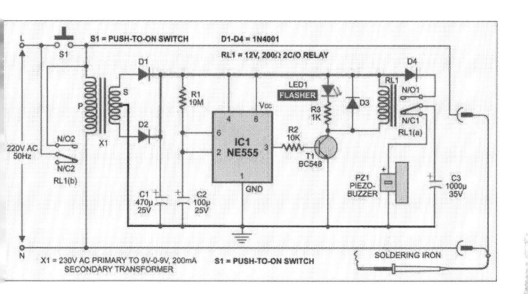

46. White LED Light Probe for Inspection

This circuit is valuable for investigating thin spaces like within the CPUs, monitors, PCB modules and other electronic gadgets. The light source is a pencil thin tube with ultra-bright white LED at the tip.

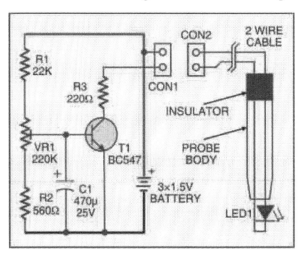

47. Calling Bell Using an Intercom

Here is a basic calling bell circuit that can be utilized as a part of small offices to call the office boy utilizing a current intercom system. The office boy can be called from up to 9 locations where addition lines are installed. The system is associated with a dedicated extension for the office boy. At whatever point somebody needs the office boy's assistance, he can dial the office boy's addition number through the intercom and then press a key to indicate his location number (say, 5). This number will be displayed on a 7-segment display and at the same time a bell will sound to alert the office boy. Pressing a button or switch will be clear the display.

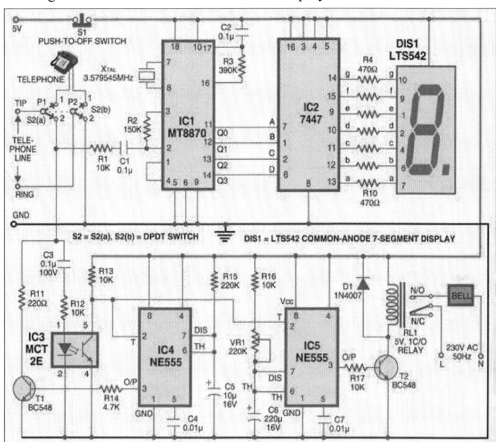

48. FM Bug

This FM bug transmitter circuit will give you a chance to spy on individuals. The transmitter can be put in the coveted room and the discussion got notification from a place far away simply utilizing a general FM radio set.

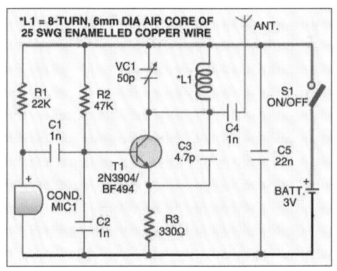

49. Digital Frequency Comparator

This is a digital frequency comparator for oscillators that shows the outcome through a seven-segment show and a LED. At the point when the frequency tally of an oscillator is beneath '8,' the relating LED stays turn-off. When the tally achieves '8,' the LED turns on and the 7-segment show indicates '8'.

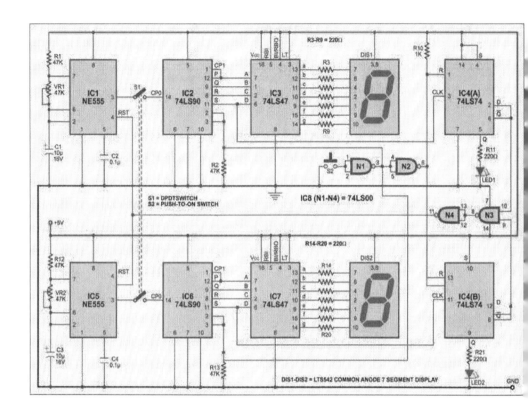

50. Bhajan and Mantra Chanting amplifier

Individuals in India get a kick out of the chance to serenade different mantras as they trust it brings good luck, peace of mind and aides in concentration. Here we introduce the circuit of an electronic chanting gadget having nine bhajans and one mantra to look over.

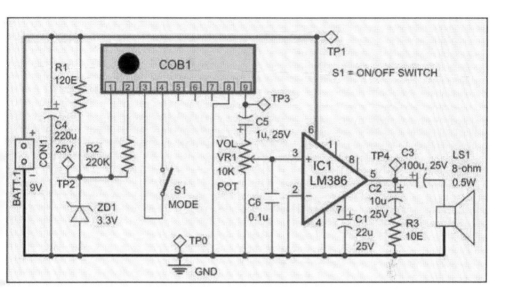

51. Quality FM Transmitter

Here's FM transmitter for your stereo or somewhat other amplifier delivers a good signal strength up to a distance of 500 meters with an energy output of about 200 mW. It works off a 9V battery.

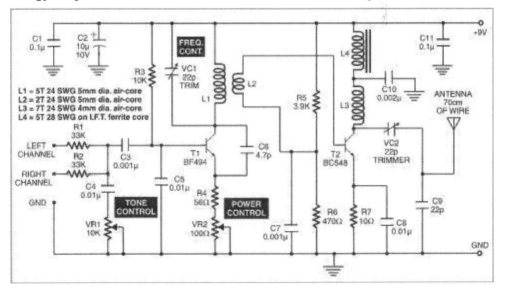

52. Mains Box Heat Monitor

This basic circuit monitors the mains dispersion box always and sounds an alarm when it detects a high temperature because of overheating, anticipating disasters caused by any starting in the mains box because of short circuits. It additionally naturally switches on a splendid white LED when the power comes up short. The LED gives adequate light to check the mains box wiring or wires in obscurity. The circuit beeps once when control comes up short and again when control resumes.

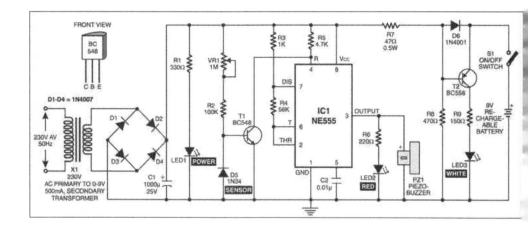

53. Tachometer

A tachometer is a device used to measures the rotational speed of a pole or disk in a motor or other machine. Here we introduce the fundamental variant of the tachometer that demonstrates the revolutions per second (RPS) on an advanced show.

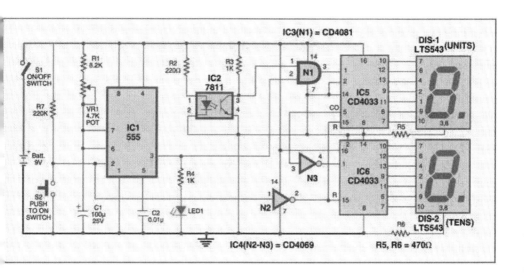

54. Timer from Old Quartz Clock

You can manufacture an exact, cost efficient timer from the circuit of an old quartz clock. This timer has a time duration of up to two hours, which is adequate for most everyday activities.

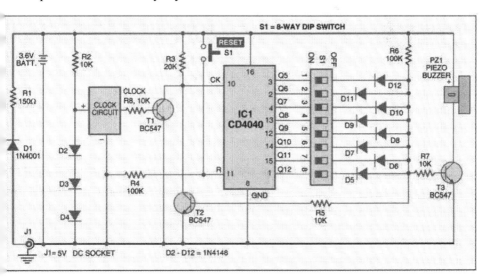

55. Keep Away Ni-Cd from Memory effect

Nickel–Cadmium batteries suffer from associate undesirable memory result because of partial discharge. The remedy is to utterly discharge the battery before recharging.

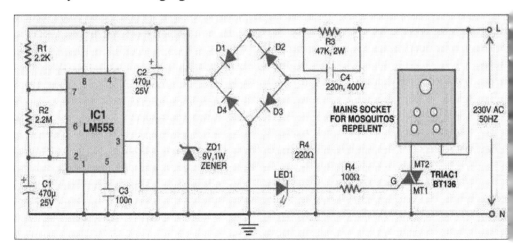

56. Periodically on off Mosquito ad hoc circuit

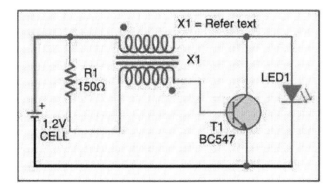

A portion of the mosquito repellents accessible in the market utilize a toxic fluid to create poisonous vapors keeping in mind the end goal to repulse mosquitoes out of the room. Because of the continuous arrival of poisonous vapors into the room, after 12 pm the natural balance of the air composition for good health comes to or surpasses the basic level. Generally, these vapors assault the brain through lungs and apply an anesthetic impact on mosquitoes and also other living creatures by little or more prominent rate. Long introduction to these toxic vapors may cause neurological or related issues.

57. Crystal AM Transmitter

This is the circuit of a medium energy AM transmitter that will pass 100-150 mW of radio frequency (RF) energy.

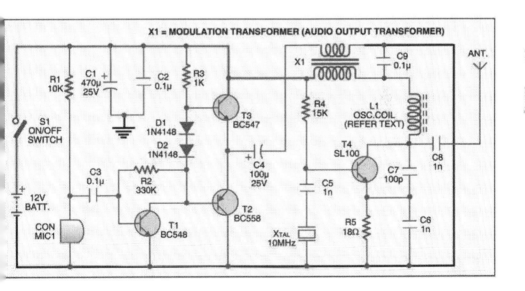

58. Programmable Electronic Dice

This is a fundamental programmable electronic dice with numeric show. This dice can be modified utilizing a 4-way Plunge switch to show any arbitrary number in the vicinity of '1' and "2," '1' and "3,"... or on the other hand '1' and "9."

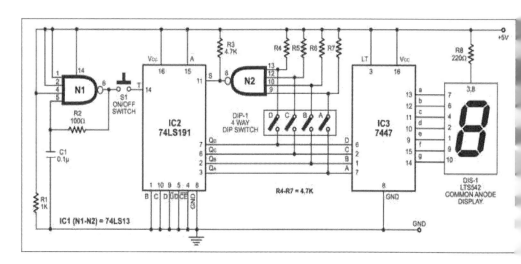

59. PC-Based Candle Igniter

This is a computer-based firing system that lets you fire up a candle using matchsticks by just pressing the "Enter" key on the Computer's keyboard. It is mostly useful when celebrating such occasions as Birthdays Celebration.

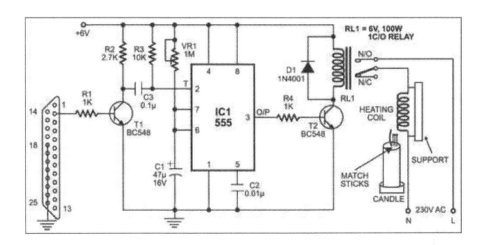

60. Sound Operated Intruder Alarm

At the point when this burglar alarm distinguishes any sound, for example, that made by opening of a door or embeddings a key into the lock, it begins blazing a light and sounding a discontinuous sound alarm to caution you of an intruder. Both the light and the alarm are naturally turned off by the following sound pulse.

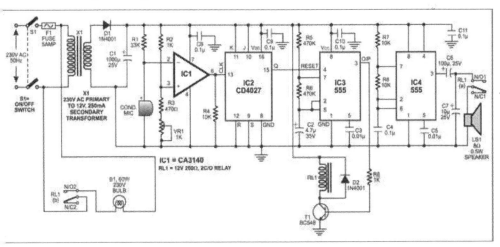

61. Versatile LED Display

This circuit utilizes an erasable programmable read-only memory (EPROM) to display different light examples on LEDs. Since bicolour LEDs (including green and red LEDs) have been utilized, display is conceivable in three hues (green, red and golden).

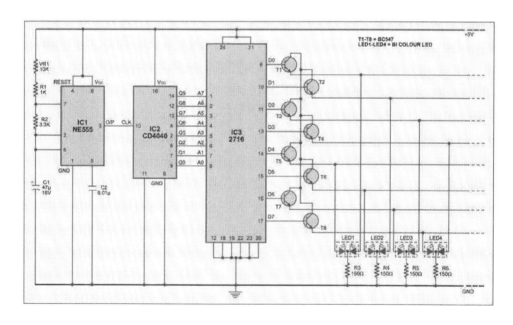

62. Multiutility flash light

This multi utility flash light comprises of three areas: a flasher, a sound-to-light show and a white LED-based flashlight.

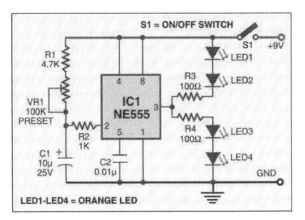

63. Twilight using white LEDs

This sunlight controlled lamp utilizes a light-dependent resistor (LDR) as the sunlight sensor and an aggregate of 25 high brilliance white LEDs. Isolate resistors are associated in series with each column of the LEDs.

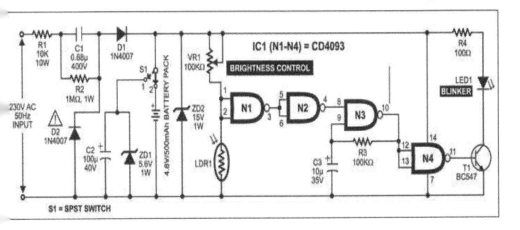

64. PC TIMER

Basically, proposed for establishment into a desktop PC, this flexible timer with movable time output gives controlled 'on' time for PC peripherals like printers, scanners and desktop perusing lamps. As it is intended for an input voltage of 12 volts, it might likewise be valuable in your lab.

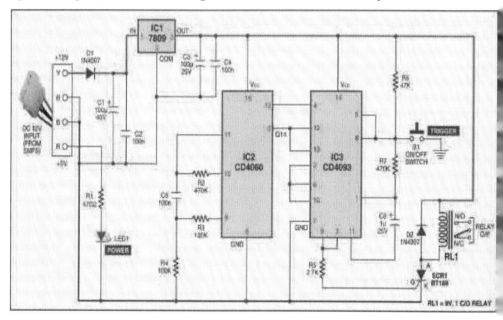

65. Infrared Object Counter

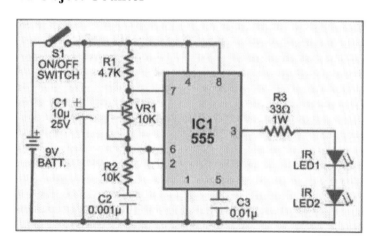

This infrared object counter can be introduced at the section gate to check the aggregate number of people entering any setting. For instance, it can be utilized at the railway stations or transport stands to check the people arriving every day or week.

66. Pushbutton Control for Single-Phase Appliances

This circuit gives you a chance to switch off and switch on a single-phase machine utilizing two separate push switches. Such a game plan is common for modern motors (generally 3-phase) where an isolation is required amongst power and control circuits. Personal protection under broken conditions is guaranteed if the transfer is put remotely. The circuit likewise defends exorbitant devices against visit power cuts as the gadget kills in case of power disappointment and stays off until the point when it is switched-on once more.

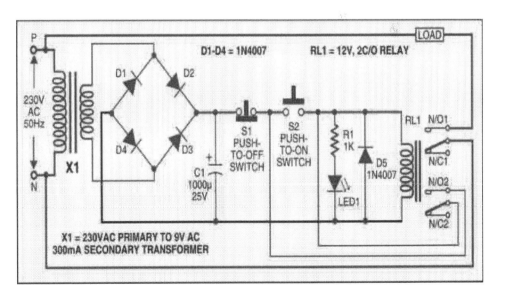

67. Soldering Iron Tip preserver

In spite of the fact that 60/40 solders melt at around 200°C, the tip temperature of a soldering iron ought to be around 370°C. This is important to make a decent joint quickly without the risk of overheating fragile components. One ought not to hold the tip of the iron to the joint for a really long time at such high temperature.

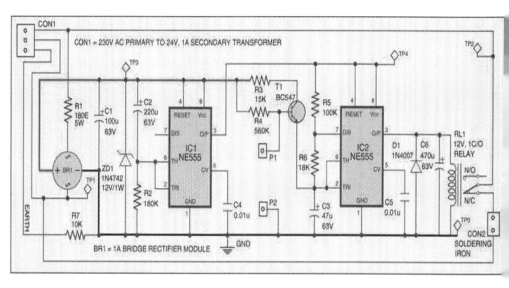

68. Over-Speed Indicator

Here's circuit is intended for showing over-speed and direction of rotation of the motor utilized as a part of small scale hand devices, water pump motors, toys and different machines.

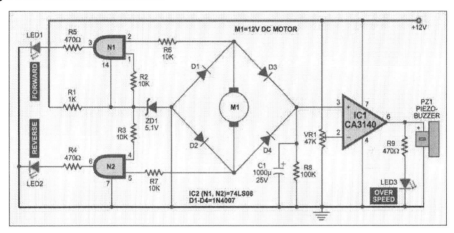

69. Automatic Washbasin Tap Controller

Influence your washbasin to tap work automatically when you put your hands just underneath the water tap outlet. This Infrared (IR)

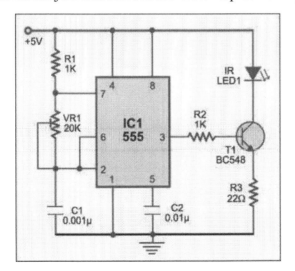

based framework detects any interference of the IR rays by your hands or utensil and water automatically begins streaming out of the tap

70. 1.5W Power Amplifier

Here we set all the theory to work and present a basic power amplifier module that can be simply worked with promptly accessible components. The block diagram of the amplifier is appeared in figure It is run of the mill of most audio amplifiers, despite the fact that the circuit is fairly unique.

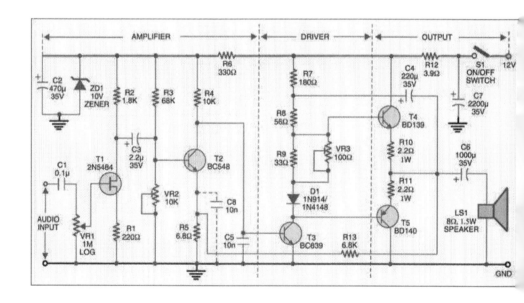

71. Wireless Stepper Motor Controllers

This is a cost efficient and basic wireless stepper motor controller using IR signals. Using this circuit, you can control the stepper motor from a distance of up to 4 meters

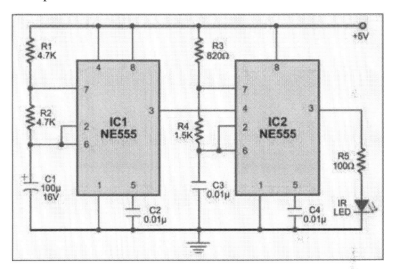

72. Battery-Low Indicator

Rechargeable batteries ought not be discharged below a specific voltage level. This lower voltage restrain relies on the sort of the battery. This basic circuit can be utilized for 12V batteries to give a sign of the battery voltage falling below the preset esteem. The sign is as a gleaming LED.

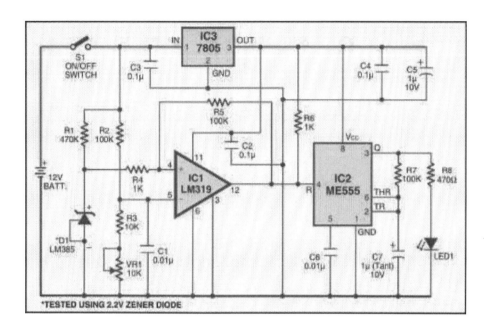

73. Speed Checker for Highways

While driving on highways, drivers ought not surpass the maximum speed limit allowed for their vehicle. Be that as it may, accidents continue happening because of speed violations since the drivers have a tendency to disregard their speedometers.

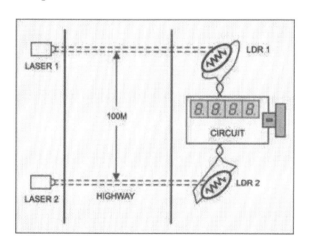

74. Simple Stereo Level Indicator

Generally, ease home stereo power amplifiers don't have output level indicators. An output power level indicator can be added to each channel of these stereo power amplifiers. As low levels of the output power are not aggravating and harming to the general humans, there is no compelling reason to include a preamplifier and low-level locator before IC LM3915. Be that as it may, you should know when the output power turns out to be extensively high.

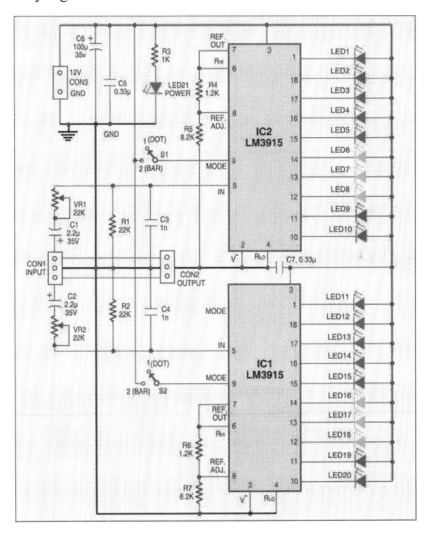

75. Manual EPROM Programmer

The programmer gadgets required for programming the electrically programmable read only memories (EPROMs) are by and high cost. This is a cost-efficient circuit to program binary information into 2716 and 2732 EPROMs.

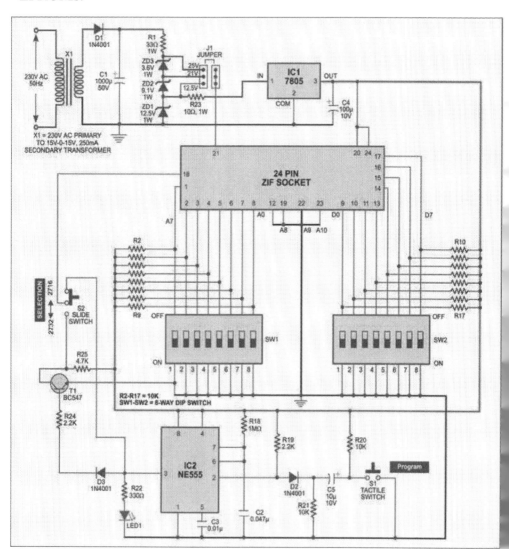

76. Noise-Muting FM Receiver

The tuning of a frequency-modulated (FM) receiver to a FM radio station frequency includes a considerable measure of 'murmuring' noise in the middle of the stations, which is exceptionally irritating for the administrator and in that capacity unfortunate.

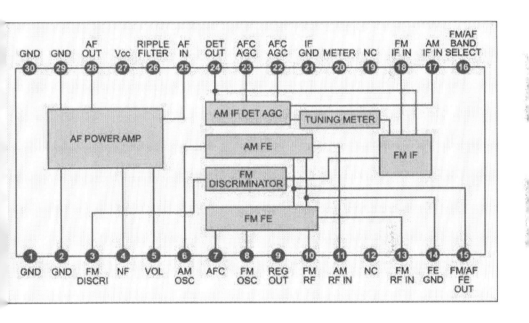

77. PC-Based Stepper Motor Controller

Here's stepper motor controller is perhaps the cheapest, littlest and easiest. A couple of H-bridges with a software program written in 'C++' is utilized to control the bipolar stepper motor with a stage determination of 18 degree per pulse.

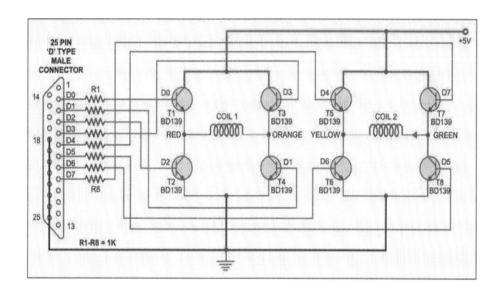

78. Digital Audio/Video Input Selector

Need to associate in excess of one Audio Video (AV) source to your shading television? Try not to stress, here's an AV input expander for your TVs. It is reasonable and simple to develop

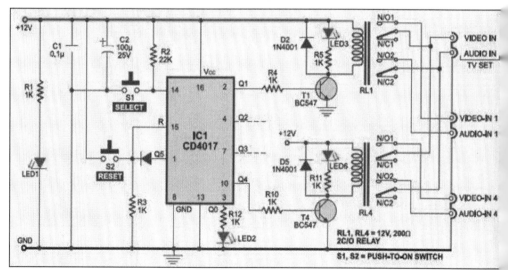

79. Automatic Bathroom Light with Back-up Lamp

Once in a while we forget to switch off the Toilet light and it stays on unnoticed for long periods. This circuit takes care of the problem of electricity wastage by switching off the lamp automatically following 30 minutes once it is switched on. The backup LED lamp gave in the circuit turns on for three minutes when mains falls flat. This is useful particularly when you are cleaning up around evening time.

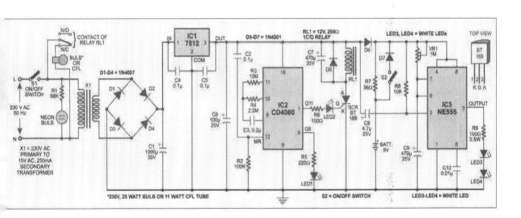

80. Simple Low-Power Inverter

This is a simple low-power inverter that converts 12V DC into 230-250V AC Power Supply. It can be utilized to power light loads like window chargers and night lamps, or essentially offer stun to ward off the gate crashers. The circuit is worked around only two ICs, to be specific, IC CD4047 and IC ULN2004.

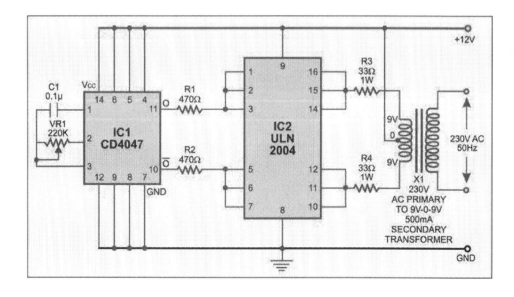

81. Mains Interruption Counter with Indicator

Here's circuit counts mains supply interruptions (up to 9) and demonstrates the number on a seven-segment display. It is profoundly valuable for automobile battery chargers. In view of the quantity of mains interruptions, the client can expand the charging time for lead-acid batteries.

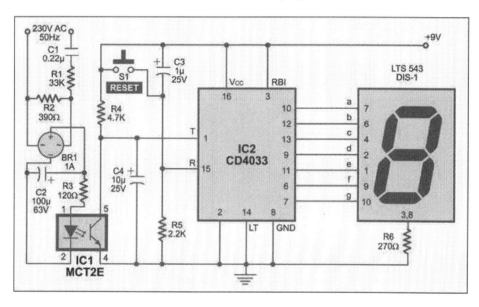

82. FM Adaptor for Car Stereo

On the off chance that your car has a FM radio with stereo yield yet no inbuilt cassette player, this circuit will come convenient for tuning in to your most loved gathering of music from your own audio player through the FM-stereo car radio.

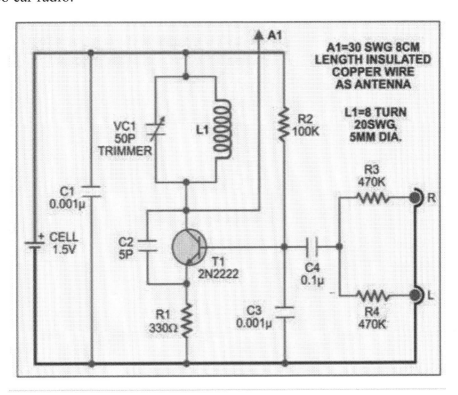

83. Panic Plate

Valuable for the elderly and feeble people, here's touch-sensitive circuit sounds a panic alarm to get the consideration of others for quick help. The touch plate settled on the wall close to the bedside gives a simple access to the individual on bedrest so he may call for assistance absent much trouble. Yellow LED3 on the board demonstrates the call and the red LED shows a quick consideration.

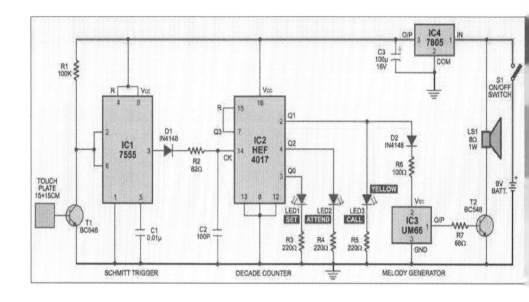

84. Twinkle X-mas Star

Christmas just would not be Christmas in the event that you don't put a flashing star in your Christmas tree. this is the circuit of like a flashing star.

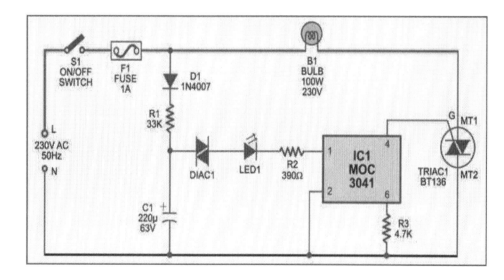

85. Car Fan Speed Controller

Utilizing this circuit, you can control the speed of 12V DC fans utilized as a part of cars. The circuit is worked around timer 555, which is wired as an astable multivibrator. The yield of the multi vibrator is nourished to IRF 540 MOSFET. The fan is associated between the +ive terminal of the battery and drain (D) of MOSFET T1. Capacitor C1 is associated in parallel to the fan to balance out its speed. Freewheeling diode D1 shields the motor from back emf. A fuse is incorporated for safety.

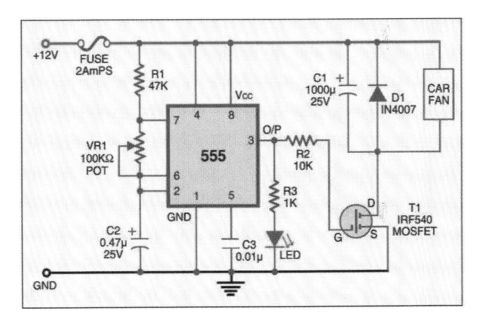

86. In Car Food and Beverage Warmer

Here's an exceptionally valuable device for the individuals who are frequently on move. It will keep your tea, espresso or food warm while consuming little power.

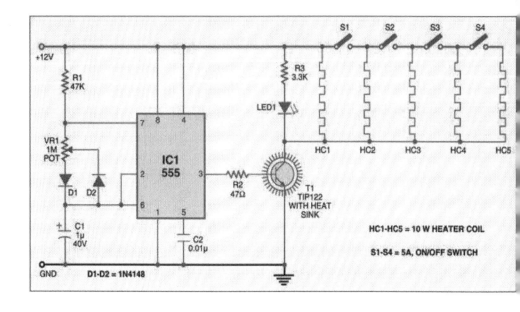

87. Three Component Flasher

Since this flasher system utilizes just three components, it is moderately simple to build and install. It can be utilized for signal flashing, peril cautioning and interchange flashing.

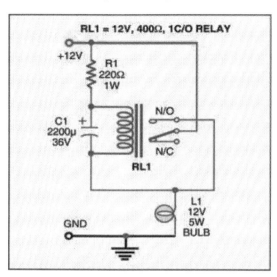

88. Night Lamp

Here's two-night lamp circuits utilizing LEDs. One could be utilized as a night-vision clock and alternate as a TV lamp. Both the circuits are AC worked and expend next to no power. These are additionally ensured against mains variances. The night-vision lamp utilizes twelve LEDs masterminded in the circular pattern of a divider clock, while the TV lamp utilizes 24 LEDs in prism design.

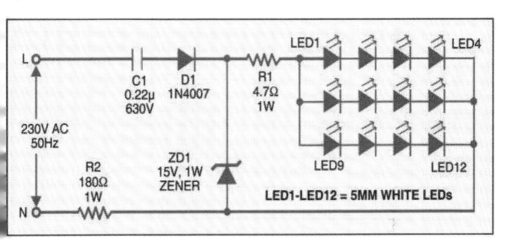

89. Hot-Water-Ready Alarm

Electric kettles turn-off consequently when water has boiled. Imagine a scenario in which the boiler beeps to alarm you when your water has boiled. The tripping sound of the thermal switch may not enroll as an alarm in your brain. Here's such an extra unit, to the point that gives irregular beeps toward the finish of bubbling. It has the benefits of to a great degree low part check, minimal effort, little size and light weight.

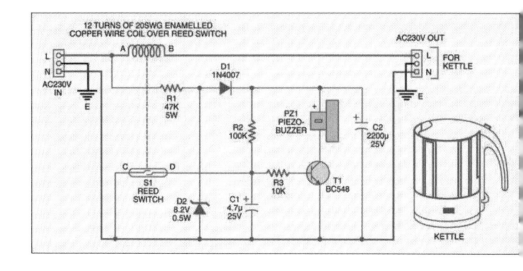

90. Optical Smoke Detector

Here's optical smoke detector utilizes a Cost Efficient, promptly accessible, opened, through-scan, infrared photograph switch. At the point when smoke is sensed, the relay stimulates to activate the audio/visual cautioning alarm.

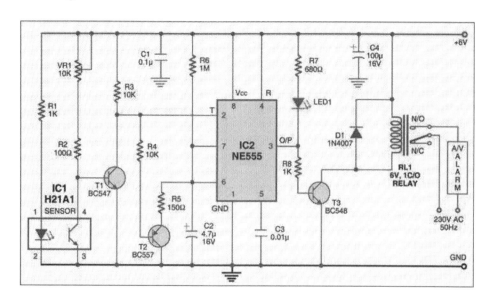

91. Capacitance-Multiplier Power Supply

This is the circuit of a Most Effective power supply with regulation that uses a Centre tapped transformer.

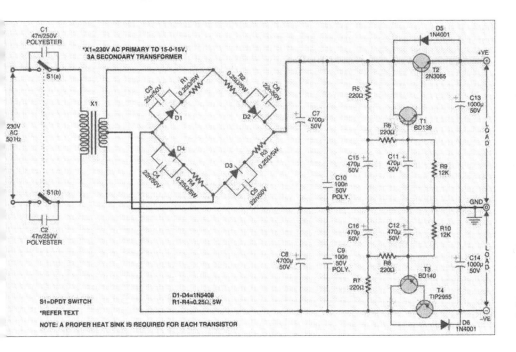

92. Wireless PA for Classrooms

In huge classrooms, numerous a times the staff's voice isn't audible to students in the back rows. So the staff need to truly yell to be heard by each understudy. Introduced this is a circuit that can go about as a wireless speech-aid for staff with the goal that their voice reaches to everyone even in a substantial classroom.

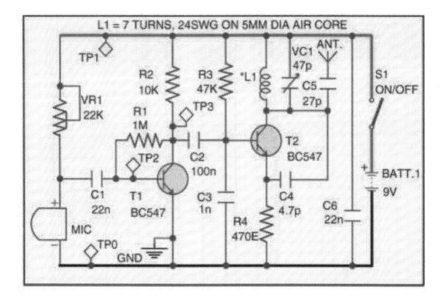

93. Low-Cost Battery Charger

This is an extremely basic and low-cost charger for 12V, 7Ah lead acid batteries. It can likewise be utilized for powering vehicle motors and crisis lighting frameworks.

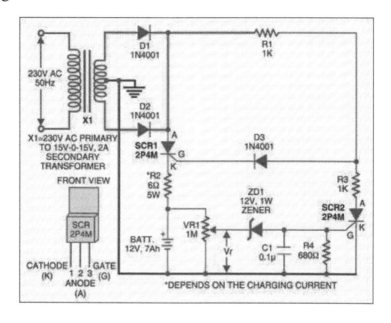

94. Simple Automatic Water-Level Controller

Water level controllers are very common in Nowadays. The one depicted here is worked around timer NE555 and inverter buffer CMOS IC CD4049. It utilizes promptly accessible, low cost components, and is anything but simply to make the circuit and install on the overhead tank (OHT) to preserve water from overflow.

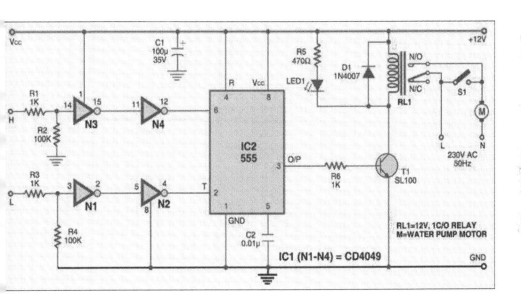

95. Touch-Plate Doorbell

Here's touch plate doorbell makes utilization of enhancement-mode MOSFETs framing some portion of CMOS quad NAND entryway CD4007B in conjunction with a detector and Darlington driver arrange.

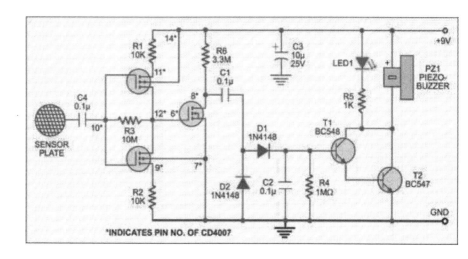

96. Electronic Ludo

Ludo, a traditional board game, requires the players to throw a dice by hand and push ahead their tokens on the board by the quantity of squares indicated by the dice. In this electronic version, the players need to press a push-to-on switch instead of throwing the six-surface dice. At the point when the switch is pressed momentarily, the seven-segment digital counter displays a number immediately. As in the manual dice, the numbers are displayed randomly in the vicinity of '1' and '6' contingent upon the time for which the player presses switch S1.

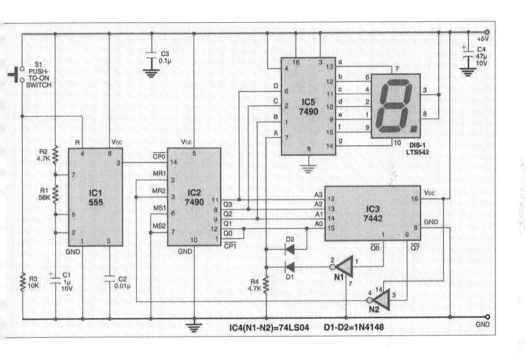

7. Motorbike Alarm

This easy-to-build alarm can be fitted in bikes to shield them from being stolen. The modest circuit can be shrouded anyplace, with no complicated wiring. Practically, it suits all bikes as long as they have a battery. It doesn't deplete out the battery however as the standby current is zero.

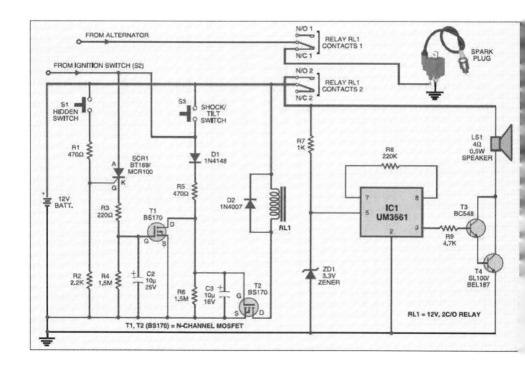

98. Dual Motor Control for Robots

Exhibited here is a basic circuit that can drive two motors for a little robot, enabling the robot to arrange an obstacle course. Two light dependent resistors (LDRs) are utilized to recognize the obstacle and the motors are driven correspondingly to maintain a strategic distance from the obstacles consequently. Two H-bridge motor circuits are utilized that can drive each motor forward or backward, or stop it, independently.

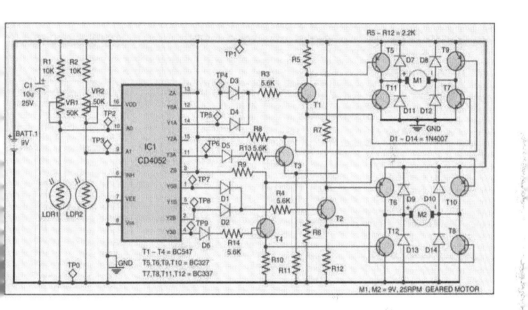

9. Environment Monitoring System Using Arduino

An agreeable environment can expand the efficiency multi folds. So, it is vital that the environment factors, for example, temperature, relative tickiness, dew point, light power and air quality (gas/smoke), are ceaselessly checked and comparing systems acclimated to keep up an open to workplace.

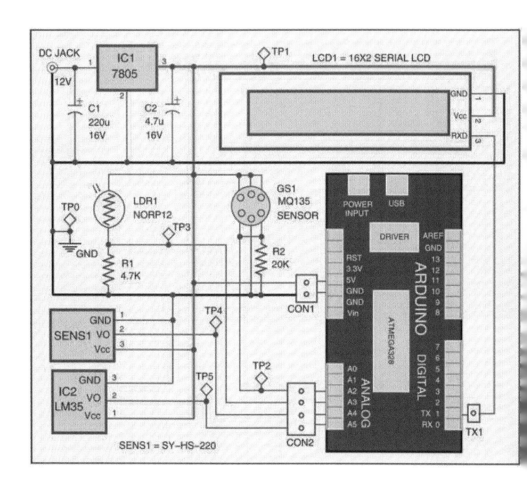

100. Long-Range IR Transmitter

The majority of the IR remotes work dependably inside a range of 5 meters. The circuit intricacy increments on the off chance that you plan the IR transmitter for dependable task over a longer range, say, 10 meters. To twofold the range from 5 meters to 10 meters, you have to increase the transmitted power four times.

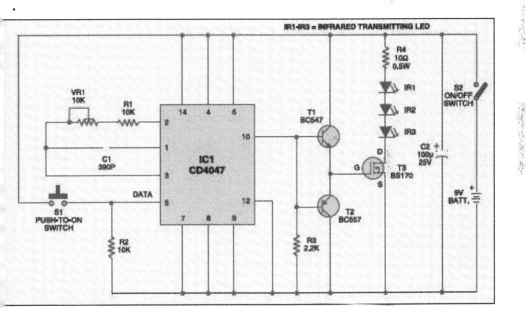

MORE USEFUL LINKS

Here are links to projects, tutorials, parts, and online communities to help you get started with *electronics projects for beginners*.

Instructables.com

Written by a thirteen-year-old, this article links to a number of mini projects geared to students new to electronics. Projects contain a how to solder, solar iPhone charger, a water energy calculator and a solar cockroach.

http://www.instructables.com/id/Electronic-Projects-For-Beginners/

http://www.instructables.com/id/Beginners-Electronics-Projects/

5 Beginner Projects That Work on The Initial Attempt

Links to videos viewing simple projects, with a clap on clap off switch.

http://www.buildcircuit.com/5-beginners-projects-that-work-in-the-first-attempt/

Simple Electronics Projects for Beginners

Articles by reader comments for a project, by a FM radio transmitter, water level indicator, and infrared motion detector.

http://www.circuitstoday.com/simple-electronics-projects-and-circuits

Electronics Projects for Dummies

No one who seen this magazine is a dummy, but this Dummies website has a great step-by-step group of projects for a coin toss circuit that also imparts the process of designing and making electronics projects.

http://www.dummies.com/how-to/consumer-electronics/electronics/Electronics-Projects.html

Beginner Electronics Projects from Radio Shack

Actually, an impression article with about ideas on what they offer student who want to get started by electronics projects, for i.e., Engineer Small Notebooks which sound interesting.

http://techchannel.radioshack.com/beginner-electronics-projects-1831.html

Electronics Projects from Makezine

While maximum of their projects is not for novices, this is a great website to browse to get enthusiastic about what you might do once you finish a few electronics projects for beginners. Here's some really arranged projects on his site.

http://makezine.com/category/electronics/

Ben Heck Show: Back to Basics

Important skills like how not to fry your projects.

http://www.youtube.com/playlist?list=PLwO8CTSLTkijrSW6DIFsQxcvjRo5fZ-y5

Spark Fun Tutorials

https://learn.sparkfun.com/tutorials

How to Solder

The ability to solder, with heat to fuse two soft-metals, is a important skill for electronics projects.

https://learn.sparkfun.com/tutorials/how-to-solder—through-hole-soldering/all

Parts for Electronics Projects

ADAFRUIT

To Concentration on Arduino, Raspberry Pi, and Beagle Board parts and projects, through lots of tutorials.

https://www.adafruit.com/

ELEMENT 14

Element 14 demonstration that features electronics projects, as well as an online free where you can get assistance by your projects.

http://www.element14.com/community/welcome

OCTOPARTS

A search engine to discovery electronic parts from various different sellers.

http://www.octopart.com/

MINIBREAD

http://www.minibread.com/

SPARK FUN

https://www.sparkfun.com/

References

1. Earl Boysen and Nacy C.Muir (2006), Electronics Projects for Dummies.
2. Cathleen Shamieh (2015), Electronics for Dummies
3. Charles Platt (2015), Make electronics Second Edition.
4. Bill Pretty (2015), Getting Started with Electronics Projects
5. http://electronicsforu.com/newelectronics/lab/freecircuitslist.asp?id=1026
6. http://electronicsforu.com/newelectronics/lab/freecircuitslist.asp?id=1028
7. http://electronicsforu.com/newelectronics/lab/freecircuitslist.asp?id=1027

About The Author

Arsath Natheem is an Indian Biomedical Engineer and Youtuber who works primarily in the field of Artificial intelligence, He is best known for his multimedia Presentation about "How the Biomedical Engineers Save the life" at Velalar College of Engineering and Technology in Tamilnadu, he was awarded the best project holder for Human Interaction Intelligence Robot as Personal Assistance, and IoT Based Voice Recognition Robot for defenses, also presented his project at Adhiyamaan college of engineering and Technology and won the first prize for his project. He participated project competition at Madras institute of technology (MIT) in Chennai, He completed his Undergraduate Degree at Velalar College of Engineering and Technology, He Interested in the field of an Artificial Intelligence that's will be specifically applicable for Medical Diagnosis.

ONE LAST THING…

If you enjoyed this book or found it useful I'd be very grateful if you'd post a short review on Amazon. Your support really does make a difference and I read all the reviews personally so I can get your feedback and make this book even better.

If you'd like to leave a review then all you need to do is click the review link on this book's page on Amazon.com

Thanks again for your support!

Made in the
USA
Middletown, DE